What Happened to Daddy's Body?

Explaining what happens
after death in words very young
children can understand

Elke and Alex Barber
Illustrations by Anna Jarvis

Jessica Kingsley *Publishers*
London and Philadelphia

From us...

To Daddy

I love you,
I will always miss you
and neverf orget you.

Alex xxx

For John - thanks for "getting it"
and always being there for us.

For Jodie, Lauren, Nicole, Alex, Leanna,
Rhiana and Olivia - love you millions!

For Mart - we miss you every day.
Thanks for having been in our lives.

For everyone who misses someone terribly.
I hear you. You are not alone. Big hugs.

Elke xxx

To Elsie, Lola and
especially David for
all your love and
encouragement.

Anna xxx

...and from some of our amazing crowdfunders. xx

To Simon,

a dearly loved
and dearly missed Daddy,
and to all those little
(and big) ones out there
who wish their daddy
could come back.

Love Lucy, Matthew,
Ella and Amelia xxxx

To William and Jaiden,
whose daddy Wes misses them
desperately and so wishes he could
be there to give them a cuddle.

And to Sarah
- one of the nicest people
I have ever been fortunate
enough to hug.

Elke xxx

For our shining star Graeme,

Our lives are enriched
through your poetry,
art and love shared
so freely.
Memories continue to
bring us comfort and
happiness now you are
no longer with us.

Forever in our hearts,
Kirsty and Ceara xxx

"In memory of my
wonderful daddy John
McLoughlin, love you
always, Lily xx"

"I have my daddy's eyes,
my daddy's lips
and my daddy's smile.
My daddy is with me always......
forever his Princess."

Stephen D. Adamson,
forever missed,
forever loved.
Tia (age 6), Ryan (age 17)
and his wife Karen

This is for Ray Franklin,

a wonderful daddy to Liam
and to the late Jack,
forever in our thoughts.

Love from your wife Angela,
Liam and Jack xxx

Hi, I am Alex.

I am
(one...two...three...)

four
years old!

I live with my mummy and
my little sister Olivia.

We have a really fun garden.

My daddy loved his garden...

He died this year.

Today Mummy, Olivia and I are making cupcakes for a picnic.

We **love** making cupcakes!

Mixing everything together is really messy, and licking the spoon is just the best!

Once they are baked,
we decorate them.

My favourite icing colour is green, and I LOVE putting
lots and lots of sprinkles on. It is great fun!

We take everything outside, and sit on our
favourite picnic blanket on the grass.

Being in the garden always makes
me think of Daddy...

"Mummy," I ask, "remember you said that Daddy can't use his body any more? Can you tell me again what happened to it?"

"Of course," says Mummy. "Remember the funeral at the crematorium?"

"Yes," I say.

"And do you remember the big wooden box?"

I nod.

"That box is called a coffin, and Daddy's dead body was inside it.

After we told our happy, funny memories of Daddy, it was put on a special lift, which took it down into the cellar of the crematorium."

"But if Daddy's body was inside the coffin, where were his head, arms and legs?" I ask.

"Once in the cellar, the coffin is carefully put into a big machine, which is very **very hot** inside. The doors get closed, and the coffin and the dead body get burned.

This is called 'being cremated'."

"And it doesn't hurt because the dead body **can't feel anything** any more?" I ask.

"That's **exactly** right, Alex," says Mummy.

"When the big machine has cooled down again,
the bits that didn't burn completely are put inside a box.
Those bits are called 'the ashes'.

After a few days, you can pick them up
from the funeral home and take them home, if you want."

So we go inside and Mummy shows me a box.
It is not very big, but it is very heavy.

"Can I look inside?" I ask.

Mummy nods, and
opens the box.

The ashes look a bit
like sand on the beach.

"Can I touch it?"
I ask.

"I guess so..." says Mummy,
so I carefully dip my finger in.

It feels all soft and
not scary at all.

We draw little
pictures in the ashes
with our fingers.
It feels nice.

Then Mummy says it's time
to put the box away again.

"Mummy," I ask, "does everybody get cremated?"
"No," says Mummy. "Some people get buried, instead.

At burials, the coffin with the dead body inside is carefully lowered into a big hole in the ground, called a grave. Remember that a dead body can't feel anything any more!

The grave is then filled up with soil, and you can plant flowers on top.

A burial can also be called a funeral.

On top of most graves, there is a big stone with the dead person's name on it. This is called a headstone. Sometimes it also shows you when the person was born, and when they died.

In Loving Memory
MARGO 'MABS' BERRYBIRD
1908 - 1953
A brilliant mother wife & artist

Most graves are in a special place called a cemetery. Sometimes people choose to bury their dead loved ones' ashes there, too."

"So what happens to the body and the coffin after it gets buried?" I ask. "Does it stay in the grave forever?"

When it starts to get cold, they go all **soft** and **crumbly** and, eventually, turn into soil. This helps new plants to grow. It's the same with a dead body.

It takes a **long** time, but after it gets buried, it slowly turns into soil and helps feed the plants and trees."

"**Wow,**" I say.

"That's really cool."

For my birthday I am having a police party.
I am really excited - my **daddy** was a policeman!

All of a sudden I feel a bit sad that Daddy can't be here. But lots of my friends are here, and John, Mummy's boyfriend, and his five children, too.

John is not my daddy, but he is very funny and I like him a lot.

We play "Hook the Robber Duck", and when it's John's turn we shoot him with water pistols.

One day, after lots of sleeps, Mummy looks a bit sad.
"I would like to spread Daddy's ashes today," she says.

"What does that mean?" I ask.

"It means," says Mummy,
"that we'll take Daddy's ashes
to a special place, and put
them on the ground,
where they can help
plants and trees to grow."

"But I don't
want to spread
Daddy's ashes!" I say.

I cry, but Mummy gives me a **big hug** and says,
"You know, spreading Daddy's ashes
doesn't mean that we will
stop thinking about him.

We can still talk about him
every day, and remember
how much he loved us
and that he didn't want to die.

We will always **love** and
miss him, and **nobody**
can **ever** replace him.

So please
don't worry."

"What do you think, Alex?" Mummy says, and shows me two little glass bottles with teeny-tiny corks in them. "I thought that, if you like, you and Olivia could fill these and keep a little bit of Daddy's ashes for yourselves as a very special memory?"

I like that, and feel much better already.

"And with some
of the ashes, we can **plant**
a **little tree** from the garden in a big pot,
which we can take with us if we ever move house.
That way, we always have something to remember Daddy with."

I like that too, so Olivia and I fill our little bottles.

Then we put our wellies on and go out into the garden.

We mix some soil and some more of the ashes in a **big** plant pot, and plant our little tree, just like Mummy said.

It's actually really good fun, and my hands go all **muddy**!

"Daddy's ashes will help the tree to grow, you know,"
says Mummy.

I smile.

I think that's really nice.

We take the rest of the ashes to a park near the railway station where Daddy and I used to watch the steam trains.

TO THE TRAINS →

We all throw some into the air.

Mummy cries a little, but Olivia and I are having great fun.

When we are done, I say, "Can we **go** now?"

"Yes," says Mummy.

"And can we come back one day?" I ask.

"Of course!" says Mum.

"Next time we can even go for a ride on the steam train."

"Yay!"

Olivia and I shout, and we **Skip** through the puddles back to our car.

I miss my daddy every day, but Mummy, John, Jodie, Lauren, Nicole, Leanna, Rhiana, Olivia and I still have lots of fun together.

About Elke

Young widow to Martin, Mummy to Alex and Olivia, happily re-married to John (and actually a Thompson now, no longer a Barber), step-mummy to Jodie, Lauren, Nicole, Leanna and Rhiana, lover of children's books and all things childish, self-employed graphic designer, public speaker, breast cancer survivor (fingers crossed) and passionate about helping young bereaved children.

About Anna

I'm an illustrator and graphic designer and this is the second book I've collaborated on with Alex and Elke. Working on this project has been sad and happy too, because death is as tough to illustrate as it is to talk about, but drawing Alex, Olivia and co. is always fun.

About Alex

Now I am ten years old. I was three when my daddy died. I miss him every day, and I will never stop missing him. I love Doctor Who, and my favourite hobby is football. I call John "Dad" now - so I've kind of got two daddies, except one of them can't be here.

DISCLAIMER:
Please note that local laws on spreading ashes may vary depending on where you live, and should be respected.